Good Grief, Charlie Brown!

Selected Cartoons from
GOOD GRIEF, MORE PEANUTS! VOL. I

Charles M. Schulz

CORONET BOOKS
Hodder Fawcett, London

First published by Fawcett Publications,
Inc., New York

Coronet edition 1969
Eighth impression 1978

Printed in Great Britain for
Hodder Fawcett Ltd., Mill Road, Dunton Green,
Sevenoaks, Kent (Editorial Office:
47 Bedford Square, London, WC1 3DP) by
C. Nicholls & Company Ltd,
The Philips Park Press, Manchester

ISBN 0 340 10788 X

Good Grief, Charlie Brown!

KRINKLE

IT SAYS HERE THAT IF A DOG'S NOSE IS WARM, HE PROBABLY ISN'T FEELING WELL..
VERY INTERESTING...
I WONDER IF SNOOPY'S NOSE IS WARM OR COLD?
WHY DON'T YOU FIND OUT?
?
YOU MEAN TOUCH HIS NOSE?! OH, NO...I COULDN'T DO THAT...OH, NO....I'D BE SCARED...
YOU MEAN WALK RIGHT OVER, AND TOUCH IT, DON'T YOU? OH, NO....I DON'T THINK I COULD EVER.. I'LL DO IT!

ZOOM!

NO, NO, SNOOPY! NOT THOSE!!

WHAM!

BOY, WHAT A STUPID DOG!

SCHULZ

WHOP!

BASEBALL IS NO LONGER A HITTER'S GAME..

THE WONDERFUL WORLD OF PEANUTS

Numbers 1–25 and all the above Peanuts titles are available at your local bookshop or newsagent, or can be ordered direct from the publisher. Just tick the titles you want and fill in the form below.

Prices and availability subject to change without notice.

〜〜〜〜〜〜〜〜〜〜〜〜〜〜〜〜〜〜〜〜〜〜〜〜〜〜〜

CORONET BOOKS, P.O. Box 11, Falmouth, Cornwall.
Please send cheque or postal order, and allow the following for postage and packing:
U.K. – One book 22p plus 10p per copy for each additional book ordered, up to a maximum of 82p.
B.F.P.O. and EIRE – 22p for the first book plus 10p per copy for the next 6 books, thereafter 4p per book.
OTHER OVERSEAS CUSTOMERS – 30p for the first book and 10p per copy for each additional book.

Name ....

Address ....

....